PRAISE FOR *HI-FIVE TO WINNING*

As I expected, *Hi-Five to Winning* perfectly captures what I needed in my younger days when I craved positive guidance and easy-to-follow action steps without the long lecture. But the best surprises in *Hi-Five to Winning* are the golden nuggets of wisdom seamlessly woven throughout that fuel self-esteem and provide those boosts that are beneficial to folks of all ages and in all stages of life and career. The T.A.P.S. model is a perfect and succinct reminder of how to win and keep on winning with Confidence at the core for continuous growth. Mr. Carr is spot on with this much needed manual!

Arnitria Shaw Whitfield | Educator, Higher Ed Administrator, DEI

What do legendary winners like Michael Jordan and LeBron James know about what it takes to win? According to success guru Jermel Carr, it's an unwavering dedication to working hard to make the most of your talent. His T.A.P.S. into Confidence formula is designed to enable anyone to boost their chances of reaching their goals by harnessing their talent as effectively as possible and building confidence. I heartily recommend the book to anyone looking to improve their ability to win.

Shawn Johal | Business Growth Coach, Elevation Leaders, Bestselling Author of *The Happy Leader*

This booklet on how to achieve your goals by experienced marketer Jermel Carr is extraordinary for the succinct way in which he imparts his wisdom. As a marketing veteran, Carr understands that, in the information age, people want to get to the heart of the matter quickly, and he does so with panache and precision. The book lays out, in easy-to-follow-language, his straight-to-the-point success formula for using your talents and ambition to drive results. A must-read for anyone looking for a handy guide to developing a winning mindset!

James C. Burroughs II | SVP Government & Community Relations, Chief Equity & Inclusion Officer

To understand what it takes to become a winner it can help to be resilient, to face and overcome challenges early in life. Author Jermel Carr grew up in a tough Chicago neighborhood, and that experience helped him harness his talent and rise as a student, a Big Ten NCAA football player, and a successful marketer. In this book, he gives back by presenting his T.A.P.S. into Confidence formula for achieving success. It succinctly explains how to put yourself in position to become a winner by following your passion and turning your talent and drive into skills you can use to be successful. A great read for anyone looking to up their game and climb the next rung on the success ladder in school, athletics, or business.

Dr. Tommy Watson | President and CEO, T.A. Watson Speaking/Coaching/Consulting, Bestselling Author

I highly recommend *Hi-Five to Winning* to anyone looking for the most efficient and surefire approach to becoming a winner. In the book, Jermel Carr uses his experience in overcoming humble beginnings to become a star college athlete. He further leveraged those lessons to enhance his skills as a marketing professional.

Hi-Five to Winning delivers a comprehensive, highly intuitive system Jermel has developed for building a winning mindset and making your dreams a reality. Grab your copy of the book today!

Justin Valentine | Sales Manager, Oracle Corporation

Don't wait to snag this book. Author and top marketer Jermel Carr uses his finely honed presentation skills to present a template for winning stripped down to the essentials. The book expertly details how concepts such as setting SMART goals, using visualization, working with a support group, and harnessing your passion can improve your ability to become a winner.

Julius Barnes | Senior Investment Manager, Invesco

I highly recommend this book to anyone who aspires to live a winning life. This book is a candid and refreshingly blunt self-help book and Jermel Carr challenges conventional self-help wisdom by encouraging readers to build a winning mindset and to make their dreams a reality.

Mr. Donald Jolly | Superintendent, Warrensville Heights City School District

DOWNLOAD YOUR FREE T.A.P.S. INTO CONFIDENCE WORKSHEET HERE!

GREAT FOR ANY SITUATION OR EVENT YOU ARE LOOKING TO BUILD YOUR CONFIDENCE IN TO WIN. UNLOCKING TALENT AND PASSION TO ACHIEVE GOALS THROUGH CONSISTENT PREPARATION HAS BEEN THE KEY SEPARATOR BETWEEN THOSE WHO RISE TO THE TOP AND EVERYONE ELSE. UTILIZE THIS WORKSHEET TO HELP BE THE WINNER YOU WERE MEANT TO BE!

WINNING ACTIVITY

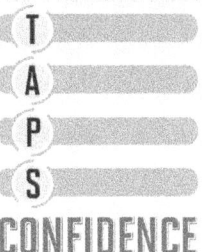

CONFIDENCE

HI-TO-FIVE WINNING
WHY WINNERS WIN

Leaders Press

JERMEL D. CARR, MBA

Copyright © 2023 Jermel D. Carr
Published in the United States by Leaders Press.
www.leaderspress.com

All rights reserved. No part of this book may be reproduced or transmitted in any form or by any means, electronic or mechanical, including photocopying, recording, or by an information storage and retrieval system—except by a reviewer who may quote brief passages in a review to be printed in a magazine or newspaper—without permission in writing
from the publisher.
All trademarks, service marks, trade names, product names, and logos appearing in this publication are the property of their respective owners.

ISBN 978-1-63735-306-6 (pbk)
ISBN 978-1-63735-246-5 (ebook)

Library of Congress Control Number: 2023914698

*This book is dedicated
to the memory of my loving mother,
Lillie Carr, who gave me confidence
that I could achieve anything
I put my mind to and was willing to work for.
And to my smart and talented son, Jelani,
Whom I work with every day
in passing that love and confidence.
They both are forever WINNERS in my book.
I also want to dedicate this book
to three key members of my inner circle
that we unfortunately lost in the last two years:
Ben, Ahmad, and Steve.*

CONTENTS

Introduction 1

Chapter One: Recognize Your Talent 5

Chapter Two: Be Ambitious 11

Chapter Three: Prepare for Success 17

Chapter Four: Identify and Leverage
                        Your Support Systems 23

Chapter Five: Have Confidence in All You Do 29

Conclusion 33

Workbook Pages 35

Acknowledgments 43

About Jermel Carr 47

INTRODUCTION

"Jermel Carr is a product of his environment." There, I said it.

People always think of this as a negative, but I'm a product of my environment, and as a marketer, I think that's a positive part of my story. I come from the south side of Chicago, and I've achieved some things that I never thought I'd be able to. Coming from a lower socio-economic background and part of the city that was grim with gangs and violence, I'm grateful to have overcome a lot of adversity and to achieve what I've achieved.

Because of that, I want to help others to have the confidence they need to achieve what they want to achieve in life.

NBA legend Larry Bird, the Hick from French Lick, famously said, "A winner is someone who recognizes his God-given talents, works his tail off to develop them into skills, and uses these skills to accomplish his goals."

I couldn't have put it better myself, but throughout this book, I'm going to try.

Winning is a mindset. It's not about coming in first place in every situation, because that's not realistic—and because some people may cheat to come in first. Winning is all about doing things the right way to put yourself in the best position to be successful and achieve your goals.

They say that when you fail to prepare, you prepare to fail. The same is true for winning. If you don't prepare to win, you're preparing to lose.

Winning is also personal, and it can be personal both to individuals and a small group or team. It also differs from person to person. Take a marathon for example: For Eliud Kipchoge, the current record holder, winning means finishing first. For a seasoned runner, winning means beating their personal best time. For someone who's running it for the first time, winning might just mean crossing the finish line. All three of them can participate in the same marathon and be seen as winners.

The principles that I share in this book aren't rocket science. My job is just to bring them together in a way that is easy to remember and provides a new way of thinking about them so that you can boost your confidence and win in the situations that matter to you the most.

We're going to highlight five major principles throughout this book as part of an approach that shows how a winner TAPS into confidence:

1. **T**alent
2. **A**mbition
3. **P**reparation
4. **S**upport
5. **Confidence**

Those first four principles all lead to having confidence, and it's the confidence that's going to make you a winner.

I've read books where people have twenty or thirty things listed that you need to be successful, which is way too many for people to remember. Instead of doing that, I've distilled everything down into these five key principles that are easy to remember, easy to use, and easy to celebrate with a Hi-Five!

Let's get started.

Chapter One

RECOGNIZE YOUR TALENT

Be Reflective and Self-Aware

Just like Maya Angelou, an American author and activist, said, "I believe that every person is born with talent." Recognizing your talent is a process, though. It's not like you just wake up one day and think, *OMG, look at all this talent I have!*

People recognize their talent by being reflective and self-aware. This is a learned skill that comes with time.

When we're kids, our parents send us to dancing and singing classes, math competitions, sports camps, or whatever else to determine what we're good at. We try different things out, and after a while, we get an idea of what our talents must be. We can do exactly the same thing as teens and adults.

It also helps if you, as an individual, know that you're really good at something. It's not enough to draw a few pictures and for your friend to say, "OMG, you're talented!" It's important to gauge yourself against others and open yourself up to feedback.

For example, I love to sing in the shower, but when I go to a concert or listen to the church choir, I can compare myself to the performers and know that I'm not a good singer. I'm self-aware enough to realize that I don't have that certain talent.

Sometimes other people will recognize your talent before you do, so it's worth listening to what people say, especially if they're someone you respect and trust or who has expertise in that area. Sure, there might be some naysayers, but part of being self-aware also requires you to know when to ignore people.

Let's take a look at an example from my own life.

As a kid, I was always fast, but I hadn't had the chance to play organized sports beyond the odd baseball or football game in the park. My chance came in my freshman year. I was walking into school on the first day of class when the high school coach came over to me and asked, "What do you think about playing football? I want you to come and try out for the team."

I hadn't really thought about it before that, but I ended up trying out, making the team, playing, and being pretty good at it. I carried on playing throughout high school and later at a major college program.

Find Your Passion

A passion is something that you want to do nearly every day and that you always find time for. It doesn't matter whether anyone's watching or not. That's what passion is about. It's when you'd do something without being graded or paid for it. It's what gets you up in the morning—something that you'll happily continue doing whether or not you get any outside stimulus for it.

Now don't get me wrong. If you can get paid for it, that's great, and you can have a passion that you get paid really well for. Typically, though, people are motivated by intrinsic value for these passions. They enjoy doing it for the sake of doing it.

It falls on you to find that passion and then hone it. Let's say that your passion is painting. Once you know it's your passion and you're already doing it, you should read up on it and understand its history. Make yourself more knowledgeable about it.

This also comes back to looking at the landscape and seeing who's doing it well. You might be able to follow in their footsteps or learn from the examples that they set. Even when something is our passion, we still sometimes need a little push to keep us going. When something is your passion, you already care about it, and you're already working on it. Back that up by putting some purpose behind the passion. After that, the sky's the limit. You can be successful beyond your wildest dreams while doing something that you love and care about.

It's like the famous and inspiring Confucius quote, "Choose a job you love, and you'll never have to work a day in your life."

Get Feedback from Trusted People

Whenever I talk to students, I tell them that if they've been doing something for five or six years, and no one has ever come up to them to tell them that they're good at it, it might be time to acknowledge that while it's something they love to do, it's not their biggest talent.

Feedback is important because even though we're talking about being internally driven and having self-awareness, we also need to understand how well we do something when we're compared with other people.

Bear in mind that you shouldn't take feedback or criticism from just anyone, especially if they have no experience or training in the area that's up for discussion. You need to make sure that you're listening to the right people. This means making sure that they have your best interests at heart. When I talk to students about taking advice from their friends, they need to remember that not all of those "friends" want them to be successful.

Sometimes the people who care about you believe in you so much that they want more for you than you even want for yourself. Listen to these people, and let them direct you toward other people who might be able to help you.

For example, if your passion is rocketry, there might be someone in your family who doesn't know much about rockets but who *does* know someone who works for NASA that they could introduce you to.

If I could distill this section down into a single message, it would be this: Don't take feedback from just anyone. If someone has never played a cello in their life, I'm not going to ask them for tips on how to play it. I'm going to find someone who's been playing it for years.

Not all feedback is created equal.

Chapter Two

BE AMBITIOUS

Continuously Set Goals

Let's talk about being ambitious and setting goals. The great athlete Bo Jackson said, "Set your goals high and don't stop 'til you get there."

I'm a big advocate of SMART goals, which are goals that are specific, measurable, achievable, relevant, and time-specific. You may have heard other variations of this, but they all boil down to the same thing: setting effective goals.

Here's how a SMART goal breaks down using the example of someone whose passion is music:

- **Specific**: Be as specific as possible, so the goal would be to "record an album" rather than "make new music."
- **Measurable**: Include measurements and metrics, so "record an album with at least fifteen tracks" rather than "record a long album."
- **Achievable**: Make sure that your goal is realistic, so "record an album with at least fifteen tracks

that my family and I can be proud of" instead of "record the world's best-selling debut album."
- **Relevant:** Ensure that your goal is relevant to you, so "record an album about past relationships with at least fifteen tracks that my family and I can be proud of" instead of "record an album that rocks."
- **Time-Specific:** Give yourself a time limit, so "record an album about past relationships with at least fifteen tracks that my family and I can be proud of by the end of July" instead of "record an album at some point."

It's important for you to write these goals down and understand how you're going to get there. You should also display them somewhere you can see them because the worst thing you can do is to put them in a drawer somewhere and forget about them. If you do that, they become DUMB (Don't Utilize My Benchmark) goals.

You should revisit them regularly and adjust them if needed. You can also add to them once you start to accomplish those goals. Most importantly, recognize and celebrate when you accomplish one of your goals, as that will give you the motivation to keep moving forward and tackle the next goal on your list.

Celebrating the milestones is also important because each one of them brings you one step closer to your final goal. Celebrating gives you a chance to breathe, enjoy your accomplishments, and reflect on what it took to get there before focusing in on whatever's next for you.

Prepare for Naysayers

When things get tough, you need to keep on pushing and stay motivated by focusing on your long-term ambitions. The key here is to make sure it's something you want for *you*, not something that you're doing to win approval from someone else. When you look back at your ambitions and goals, remind yourself why you set them and what made them important to you.

There will always be people who try to lead you away from your path and distract you from your ambitions. In a lot of cases, that's because they had similar ambitions that they couldn't achieve themselves, so they're saying that you can't because maybe they're either jaded or jealous. They don't want you to achieve things that they couldn't because you'll leave them behind.

You have to make sure that you don't allow people to push their negative thoughts and ideas onto you, because the last thing you want is a distraction. You need to focus on your end goal and keep pushing forward if you want to achieve it.

If you come from a minority group or an underprivileged background, there will also be people who've never seen someone in your position accomplish the things that you want to achieve. In those instances, you need to find your own path and have that intrinsic drive and ambition, but if you can find others who can serve as an example or an inspiration, that's even better.

In my case, no one in my family or my friends had ever graduated from college, so there wasn't an example that

I could replicate or follow. Instead of talking to them, I went to my counselor and mentor at school. They'd graduated from college, knew how to secure financial aid, and had my best interests at heart, while also providing me with a realistic opinion about what I should do.

You should also pay attention to what your end goal is. For me, it wasn't just to graduate from college. That was just a stepping stone that would help me to achieve my ultimate goal, which was to have a really good career in business so that I could get out of the neighborhood I grew up in and support my family.

When you know what your ambition is, why you set your goals, and what comes next, it becomes a lot easier to push back against the naysayers and follow your own path.

Compete with Yourself

We talked about this earlier when we touched on the idea of comparing yourself to others to understand where you are in the process and whether you've got a talent. Comparing yourself to others is good, but competing with yourself is even better when it comes to achieving your goals.

You need to have a fire within yourself that pushes you to be ambitious and reach a height that nobody thought you'd be able to achieve. You have to find that motivation, even when the days are tough, and times are hard.

When I decided to walk on to play football at the University of Minnesota, I dedicated myself to getting into the shape that I needed to be in to be successful. I had to push myself because I was taking classes and working a part-time job at UPS at the same time, but I still worked out and did plenty of training to prepare myself for what it would take to be a part of the team.

This is a useful reminder that competition isn't necessarily outside of us. We also have to find competition within ourselves. That's one of the things that I tell my son and my students. Every day, you need to figure out how to be a little bit better—not when compared to someone else, but when compared to yourself.

How can you become a little stronger, smarter, faster, or more analytical? How can you push yourself every day and become your own biggest competition?

This often comes back to the goals that you wrote down. For example, if you're preparing for a math quiz, you might say, "I did fifteen problems today, so I'm going to aim to do twenty tomorrow." Or perhaps "I ran a mile today, so I need to run a mile and a half tomorrow to get me closer to my goal of five miles."

Chapter Three

PREPARE FOR SUCCESS

Study What It Takes to Win

When you want to be good at something, it's not just a case of going out and doing it. As we've already seen, real winners learn about the history of their specialism and the people who came before them. Albert Einstein, a Nobel Prize–winning scientist, said, "Never regard study as a duty, but as the enviable opportunity to learn."

One of my good friends asks his students, "Who here wants to be a basketball player in the NBA?" A lot of the kids raise their hands. Then he asks, "Who here has read or listened to a book about basketball?" And almost all of them put their hands down. He uses this to teach them that you can't be great at something or reach the highest level if you haven't really studied it.

This research is what separates the winners from the losers. It's similar to attending an interview. I've had people come into interviews and asked them, "What have you learned or know about the company?" You'd be surprised (or maybe you wouldn't) by how many people tell me that they only read the job post or description.

That won't get you the job. You need to do your homework and know what the company is about and how it fits with what you are looking for. The same is true when it comes to studying your passion.

Note that this homework doesn't just mean reading, because there are a number of different ways to study, and everyone learns in different ways. Consider audiobooks, YouTube videos, podcasts, online courses, and more. Find what works for you.

Practice What You Learn

There's an old joke that goes, "Excuse me, how do you get to Carnegie Hall?" "You practice." Feel free to adapt that to make it more relevant to your passion. For example, "Excuse me, how do you get to Soldier Field?"

It should go without saying that practice makes perfect, or close to perfect. Just because you know about something and you've read up on it, it doesn't mean you can go out and do it and be successful. If that were the case, everyone who reads about and watches basketball would be playing in the NBA.

To be impactful, you need to take the knowledge, talent, and skills that you have and turn them into action by practicing, which I define as the continuous repetition of an action with the goal of getting better at it.

There's a big difference between knowledge and skill, and I'd argue that skill is the ability to put knowledge into practice. It's all about taking what you've learned, seen, and studied and turning it into an action.

Knowledge is knowing how to do something, and skill is being able to physically do it. Knowing how to put on muscle at the gym is very different from actually going and doing it.

An important thing to note here is that besides practicing physically, you also have to practice mentally. Studies have shown that by visualizing an action in your mind, you can actually get better at performing that action.

Visualize yourself being successful, whether that's by acing an interview or crossing a finish line. We've all heard sayings like, "If you can see it, you can achieve it." This speaks to the idea of our mental and physical selves working together to prepare us for success.

Be Deliberately Consistent

I'm going to go back to football for this one.

My defensive coach used to tell us, "If you have to think about it, and not just react, you're already too late." I remember one of the first games that I had a chance to play in. We weren't just beating our opponents—we were shutting them out. I was playing defense, but the person I was supposed to be covering had shifted position. While I stood there, figuring out who I was supposed to be covering, I realized that the guy had just scored a touchdown.

The interesting thing about this is that it shows how we can learn from our mistakes. I went back to my playbook and studied it over and over again, because I didn't want to get caught in a situation where I was thinking instead of reacting again.

I find that in most situations where people are successful, they've put themselves in a situation where they don't have to think—they can just react. This is especially true for athletes and musicians. The reason seasoned musicians can improvise is that they've done it over and over again until it became second nature.

That's where being deliberately consistent comes into play. This kind of stuff doesn't just happen by accident.

I once saw a video where Michael Jordan said something like, "When I was on the court, I didn't have to think about what I was going to do. There was no fear or anything about me not being successful or not knowing what I was going to do, because I did it so much in practice that I didn't have to think about it when I was on the court."

In other words, he became one of the greatest basketball players the world has ever seen because he practiced so much that when a situation came up in a game, he didn't have to think. Instinct took over, and magic happened.

This is what happens across a bunch of different areas, from chess games, interviews, to tests, etc. Now this might be my inner nerd coming out, but I love it when you take a math test, look at a problem, and know right away how to solve it because you've practiced the formula and problems multiple times.

That's another great example of deliberate consistency coming into play. It means that you don't have to sit there figuring things out because you've done it so often that your instinct kicks in.

Chapter Four

IDENTIFY AND LEVERAGE YOUR SUPPORT SYSTEMS

Build on Existing Bonds with Your Internal Support System

The renowned ballerina Misty Copeland said, "Anything is possible when you have the right people there to support you." Your support system is a group of people that's aligned with you and focused and dedicated to accomplishing some of the same goals that you want for yourself. Whether that goal focuses on you individually or on a broader team, your support systems all want the same outcome and are working together to make it happen.

You never see people at awards ceremonies saying, "I want to thank *me* because I won this award all by myself. I was the only one who did anything." Instead, they thank the people in their lives who lifted them up and gave them inspiration, information, and direction. In other words, their support system.

Your support system can show up even when you're not asking for help. They're the people who are there with you, fighting in your corner, whether you ask them to or not. They can be friends and family members (your internal support system) or people who are unrelated to you and may be new to your life (your external support system).

Not every family member is going to be a part of your support system, though. You might have people in your family who don't believe in you. Fortunately, it's easy to recognize the people who *do* support you because they'll show up at all of your events or find ways to help you out.

These people usually make themselves identifiable, and you need to be willing to receive the help that they offer. Sometimes we block people out, and sometimes people act like they want to help but are actually trying to piggyback on our success. Usually, though, we can spot when people have a genuine desire to help us with no desire to get anything out of it.

Take my son for example. I'm proud to be a part of his support network, and I know that the best way for me to do that is to help him to focus on the things that are important to him and those things that will help him to be successful.

That means helping him with his homework, getting him to his basketball practices, and being there in the audience when he's doing a live performance. He knows that I'm going to be there to help him, and that means he can go out and do what he needs to be successful in whatever areas he's passionate about.

Enhance Connections with Your External Support System

Members of your external support system come in many different forms. They could be counselors, coaches, coworkers, or church members. They're the people who help you accomplish the things you want to accomplish, and just like your internal support system, you'll be able to identify them because they'll make themselves identifiable.

One of the best ways to tap into your external support system is to be humble and willing to listen. Don't go into situations thinking that you already know everything or that you're the expert.

Sometimes, even when you know that people are in your corner and they want the best for you, you might not want to listen because you feel like you're already at a high level. Just remember that no matter what level you're at, you can still be taught, you can still be helped, and you can still be supported.

You've probably noticed by now that Michael Jordan is one of my favorite athletes. I've watched a lot of his growth and success, and I've gone out of my way to learn from him.

He was already a budding superstar when he changed coaches from Doug Collins to Phil Jackson, but even though he was already performing at an all-star level, he knew he hadn't reached his pinnacle. He had to humble himself and listen to what his new coach had to share with him, and that was what helped him to get to the next level—to be able to grow and trust his teammates instead of always relying on just himself and going one-on-one.

Besides being humble, you also need to trust the people who are next to you and know that they're going to do their job. You also need to know that they're going to help you and the team to grow. There's a level of trust that you need to have that they're going to help you and provide you with the information and tools you need to succeed.

Understand Your Group Dynamics and Roles

Going back to Michael Jordan and throwing LeBron James into the mix, these are two of the greatest basketball players of all time, but neither of them could win a championship by themselves. They needed teammates who could play specific roles.

In other words, as important as it is for them to know their own roles, they also needed to understand that they're working with other people toward a common goal.

With the Bulls, for example, not everyone could be Jordan. Dennis Rodman wasn't the leader of the team, but he was the leader when it came to rebounding and defense during the team's second three-peat.

Sometimes you have to redefine your understanding of your own role. In the case of LeBron James, as well as changing his idea of what a team was, he actually went to a different team to understand what a leader does and how a leader leads his team. He was able to take that learning and apply it to win his first championship and other championships afterward.

So it's super important to understand how to play different roles and what your role is on the team. This is just as true for the corporate world as it is for the basketball court.

Chapter Five

HAVE CONFIDENCE IN ALL YOU DO

Exercise Good Faith and Trust in Yourself

A quote from Former First Lady Michelle Obama goes, "Your success will be determined by your own confidence and fortitude." Exercising good faith and trusting yourself means going out knowing you're going to do your best no matter the situation or who your competition is.

Don't get me wrong. You need to know your competition and what they are planning to do. You need to know both their strengths and weaknesses and your own strengths and weaknesses, as well as what you've done to prepare, and more importantly, who you have in your corner.

Trust in the work you've done and the people you've surrounded yourself with. Trust that you have the skills and abilities that you need. This will lead you to be able to put your best foot forward in whatever it is that you're going to do.

You also need to have faith in the fact that success doesn't always mean you're going to come in first place. You don't have to come in first, but you do need to believe that you've been put in these situations for a reason and that learning from these experiences is a form of winning.

Learn from whatever you experience and trust what you've done to get to that point. I look at the University of Alabama football team and think that while they don't win every time, they're always in the hunt for a championship because they always take something away from their experiences that they apply the next time around or the next season.

That means that they're always confident because when they go into these situations, they know they've prepared, they've worked hard, and they're ready to learn from those situations whether they win or lose.

So when I talk about exercising good faith and trusting in yourself, it's all about remembering that you've been put into each situation for a reason. You've done the work and given yourself the best possible chance for a positive outcome.

Have Confidence versus Arrogance

People often confuse arrogance with confidence, but for me, the difference is crystal clear. Confidence is all about going out and expecting to be successful as an extension of that good faith and trust in yourself because of the work you've done.

Arrogance is different because that's what happens when you go out expecting to win or be successful just because you think you're better than other people. You'll find that most arrogant people don't put in the work because they don't think they need to.

Confidence is all about respecting yourself and your competition and acknowledging what you've done to get where you are. Arrogance is all about disrespecting your opponents and their craft and discounting the work that they've done.

This takes us full circle back to internal and external factors, because confidence is internal and is all about what you've done and why you deserve to be where you are. Arrogance is more external and tends to revolve around people thinking that they're better than other people.

To stay humble while being confident and avoid arrogance, remember that you don't know the work that other people have put in or the sacrifices that they've made along the way.

Visualize Success Based on Confidence

Arthur Ashe, an American tennis legend, once said, "One important key to success is self-confidence. An important key to self-confidence is preparation." This all goes back to what we've talked about when it comes to mental preparation. If you want to be successful, you need to visualize yourself achieving some of the things that you want to achieve. You need to see it to be able to achieve it.

If you're going into an interview, you need to see yourself getting the job. If you're in a race, you need to see yourself crossing the finish line. If you're giving a presentation, you need to see yourself receiving a rousing ovation at the end.

This ties back to the confidence you'll feel when you know you've put in the work, and you've done everything you can to prepare yourself. The only difference is that now you need to mentally visualize it and see it happening.

This isn't arrogance, because as we've already covered, that visualization is warranted because you've identified your talent, you've been ambitious in setting your goals, you've prepared to win, and you've tapped into your support network.

Visualization leads to realization, and it's not something that you do without merit. Otherwise, you're just dreaming. You need to follow each of these steps, and then turn to visualization once you've put in all of the groundwork.

If you're struggling with visualization, ask someone in your support network to help you. This comes back to the idea of surrounding yourself with people who can help you to be successful.

Proverbs 27:17 reads, "As iron sharpens iron, so one man sharpens another." In practical terms, this means that if you're the smartest person in the room, you need to go into a different room. You need to find people who can push you to get better, and then you can return the favor to them.

One of the best ways to do that is to work together on visualization and build each other up so that you all have the confidence you need to win.

CONCLUSION

We've been talking about what it takes to win, so let's flip that coin and look at what it means to lose or fail. For me, the easiest way to fail is to not set goals and not put in the work. If you're not putting yourself in a position where you can win, you're setting yourself up for failure.

This happens to all of us from time to time. For example, I've put myself in situations where I knew I wasn't going to be successful because I didn't feel confident. I was supposed to be developing a presentation for an interview, but I had some other distractions going on, so I waited until the last minute. Even as I went into the interview, I knew I wasn't going to get the job because I hadn't done the things I needed to do to be confident and successful.

But let's refocus on winning, and at the risk of repeating myself, I think it's important to remind you that winning isn't always about coming in first place. Winning is all about accomplishing a goal or putting yourself in the best position to be able to do so because of the work you've done and the belief you have in yourself and your team.

Remember that this process of winning is all about how someone TAPS into confidence:

Hi-Five to Winning

1. **T**alent
2. **A**mbition
3. **P**reparation
4. **S**upport
5. **Confidence**

I use the TAPS method because that helps people to remember each of the first four steps and how they all lead to confidence.

The main reason why I wanted to write this book is that when I look at kids and young people from backgrounds similar to mine, I can see that they often already feel defeated going into certain situations. They don't have that confidence in themselves and feel like they're unprepared. They often feel that they don't have the right tools or they're not from the right background to win.

I want them and others to have access to these principles so that they can go into situations and say that regardless of where they came from, they have the tools they need to win. I'm lucky because I've had people in my corner that have helped me, and are still helping me, along my journey, and so now I want to pay it forward to my readers.

You have everything you need to win in any situation and in life. Now it's up to you to put what you've learned into practice and become the winner that you were meant to be. Good luck, and Hi-Five!

WORK PAGES

These pages are intended to help you apply some of the concepts in this book to your own environment, consider what steps you need to take to move forward, and record your own thoughts and insights.

Talent Work Page

> "I believe that every person is born with talent."
> —Maya Angelou, American author and activist

What do you believe your top talents are?

_____

_____

_____

_____

_____

Hi-Five to Winning

Which of your skills are you most passionate about? How do you know?

_____

_____

_____

_____

_____

Ambitions Work Page

> "Set your goals high and don't stop 'til you get there."
> —Bo Jackson, two-sport professional athlete

What are your top ambitions that you want to achieve for the talent you are passionate about?

_____

_____

_____

_____

_____

What SMART goal will help you achieve your biggest ambition for that talent?

Specific

_____

Measurable

_____

Achievable

_____

Hi-Five to Winning

Relevant

_____

Time-Specific

_____

Preparations Work Page

> "Never regard study as a duty, but as the enviable opportunity to learn."
> —Albert Einstein, Nobel Prize–Winning scientist

What are you reading, listening to, or studying to help you learn more about what you are passionate about?

_____

_____

_____

_____

_____

What does your practice routine consist of? What would you like it to be?

_____

_____

_____

Support Work Page

> "Anything is possible when you have the right people there to support you."
> —Misty Copeland, Renowned American ballerina

Who would you consider as key members of your internal support system?

_____

_____

_____

_____

_____

Who would you consider as key members of your external support system?

_____

_____

_____

_____

_____

Confidence Work Page

> "Your success will be determined by your own confidence and fortitude."
> —Michelle Obama, former first lady of the United States

What are the top reasons that you believe that you have confidence?

_____

_____

_____

_____

_____

What are the top ways that you could or do exhibit confidence?

_____

_____

_____

_____

ACKNOWLEDGMENTS

I remember when I was working at a multibillion-dollar food company as a marketing manager, and I was walking some big-time consultants who were from my hometown of Chicago down to the lobby, and they asked me where I was from. I told them that I was originally from Chicago as well. Of course, that led to them asking the typical question: "Which side?" I proudly responded, "South side." After telling them that I'm a White Sox fan and answering a few more of their questions, I explained that I lived the first part of my youth in the Ida B. Wells Projects and then in other places on the south side, en route to graduating from Lindblom Technical HS. I can remember one of them stopping and looking me dead in the eye with a perplexed look on his face and asking me "Well, how did you get here?"

I proceeded to tell him that I went to Minnesota for undergrad and graduate school and then took a job in Wisconsin after that. Before I was finished talking, he interrupted me, saying, "No, how did you make it from Ida B. Wells to becoming a marketing manager at one of the top food companies in the world?" I paused, and as I pondered over the question, he said that he meant no disrespect by the question and that I should be very proud of what I had accomplished in my life and career to that point. I thanked him for the compliment and shared with him some of the things that I felt had helped me to get to that point, which were faith, determination, and support, to name a few. I realized later that this exchange would be the seed for this book.

So that's where I will start my thank-yous and acknowledgments. Thank you to those consultants for asking me that very poignant question. Thank you to all of those who led me to that point and helped shape me. The communities and elementary schools that I grew up in, my high school where "Excellence Prevails," and my university that taught me many lessons about working hard and building successful habits in and out of the lecture halls.

Of course, with internal and external support being so integral to this book and the winning process, I have to thank all of the people who have supported me in bringing this book to fruition.

Thank you to my friends, especially my Possee members who have supported me in many of my endeavors, including this one. Thank you all for always being there and pushing me to keep going.

Thank you to my mentors who have inspired me through the years, especially the two who were the first to encourage me to write this book: Tommy and Tawana. Thank you for not only pushing me to write this book but suggesting other potential ones as well.

Thank you to my fraternity brothers, especially those in my inner circle who epitomize the verse "iron sharpens iron," so a friend sharpens a friend. Thank you all for supporting me in more ways than one. Ever since I started talking about this concept and possible book, you all have supported me in any way possible. And I appreciate your true friendship.

Last, but certainly not least, I want to thank my family who have not only supported me through this process but also inspired me throughout my life. My sister and brothers especially along with my mom, who I hope is looking down on me and this book with pride. A special thanks to Jelani and Morenike for being my sounding boards, feedback providers, and key accountability partners for getting this book done and across the finish line.

I know that the support system is usually the most underrated part of the winning process, so that's why I want to be sure to acknowledge mine for helping me through this process. You all have allowed me to tap into my confidence.

Thank you!

ABOUT JERMEL

Jermel Carr is a veteran marketer and the founder and chief solutions provider of Prōject FORWARD Marketing Solutions, LLC. Formed in 2010, Prōject FORWARD is a minority business enterprise (MBE) that has been focused on providing strategic and tactical marketing solutions to practical entrepreneurs and small to mid-sized businesses to help them reach their highest branding, sales, and volume potential. From the same premise, Prōject FORWARD has developed the Personal Brand Coaching Academy program to develop curriculum, activities, and programming for students and professionals to help them understand the importance of, and how to develop, their personal brands to allow them to be as successful as possible now and in the future.

Jermel has spent over two decades in marketing. He has worked for well-known companies and brands such as Kimberly-Clark, where he worked his way up to a brand manager on the Huggies Brand, and Nestlé Prepared Foods, where he worked on the billion-dollar-plus brands of Lean Cuisine and Stouffer's.

Jermel is from the south side of Chicago, IL, where he was born and raised. He is a double graduate of the University of Minnesota, Carlson School of Management, where he earned his Bachelor of Science in Business Degree and his Master of Business Administration Degree in Marketing. A proud twenty-five-year--plus member of Omega Psi Phi Fraternity, Inc., Jermel also walked on, lettered, and played multiple years of football as a Golden Gopher. When he is not being a passionate marketer, Jermel, who resides in the Cleveland, Ohio, area, also runs a small motivational t-shirt business called Uplift Tees. He enjoys being a motivational speaker to students and professionals, trying new restaurants and cuisines, analyzing television commercials, and watching sports with—and cheering on—his teenage son, Jelani.

www.ingramcontent.com/pod-product-compliance
Lightning Source LLC
Chambersburg PA
CBHW061751070526
44585CB00025B/2865